Dirt Poetry

Benjamin Jackson

Published by Griotgraph LLC, 2025.

DIRT POETRY

Published by Griotgraph LLC

Print ISBN: 979-8-218-64292-1

This book is dedicated to the siblings and cities that shaped me:

To James, Robert, Edward, Roshawndra, Reynard, & Linda

To Zachary, Artemus, Amos, Jimmy & Mitchell

To Uniontown, Mobile, Selma, Montevallo, & Birmingham

Table of Contents

bury me in a small town where locals breed catfish,
the elders elect to store savings in their mattress,
things always fall apart, and green grass grows in patches

I can't say I'm from the streets
it was the dirt that raised me

the theatrics of backyard banter were
scholastic in ways book-learning wasn't,
and I loved sidewalk-less suburbs; everyone's
momma had sweet potatoes stocked in cupboards
still, some spirit pulls me from the dirt that raised me
and yet city me is unfamiliar

city me latches onto hip-hop classics and tries to
find identity within the syllables of streets I
never walked at night, at night
we'd go play in dark pastures
where starlight would reflect off of our innocence onto
broken beer bottles before fading into ambiance

the dirt that raised me was medicinal
if you rub the minerals in just right

the potholes stuck out like hungry hands, and
sands from hourglasses seem suspended
in time, we grew from boys to older boys

the dirt that raised me never spared the rod
and was mindful of when streetlights came on
the dirt that raised me expects homecoming

Concrete Seas

When I was a child, we lived in an apartment complex
separated from project housing
by a vast parking lot—a sea
of concrete littered with glass and candy wrappers.

In the afternoons, a host would cross the sea,
distinctly Blacker-than-we, though mostly light-skinned
and redbone compared to our milk chocolate and onyx.

We met them in the field behind my building,
exchanging traditions that made us realize we were kin.
We played games of survival.
The big gray cube was base,
and the patches of dirt were lava,
even in the winter months.

They told us of their churches,
of how even they were given dollars
just to place in plates at the end of the aisle.
Their congregation yelled at the same open space
while they passed notes written on programs down the
pews.

Their leader, Mack, says I talk white.
Mack claimed authority based on things
we'd all done or would do.
His daddy let him drink once—
sip of Bud in a smoke-filled room
littered with sunflower seed shells.
He claimed to be a different breed of nigga.
"My daddy sold drugs just to feed us,
and I got the new Jordans coming in next week."

I often wondered why my mother
only shopped at stores like Payless and JCPenney,
but I knew better than to ask how she spent her money.
My tongue remained tucked in my mouth,
and my Lugz firmly on the ground.

"You'll never beat us in kickball, homie.
Cool down before I heat up."

Niggas don't talk white like me.
He challenged me for my place within my own people.
Knocked me to the dirt and snatched my shoelaces loose.
If I stand, he will push me again.
I stand anyway.

When my mother asks why my pants are dirty,
I tell a half-lie and say I fell.
I cannot mention the push
because my mother had rules about fighting.
The first was "No fighting."
The second, "Don't get two ass-whoopings in one day."
Bae Sista said, "Win or lose, ya Black ass gotta come
home."

I wondered if I could ever be a nigga like Mack.
If someone would teach me to spit sunflower seeds,
or if a ball could feel the difference in our shoes.
I wonder how Mack and his people
could cross the sea with no cuts or gashes to be seen.
If they had ever fallen, ever been pushed to the ground.
If his daddy would beat him if he lost.

One of these head-ass children
tried to ease me
into those dirty thirteens,
but my uncles
raised a muthafucka, boy—

downright hazed a
muthafucka, boy.
We strung up and hung each
other out with no malice.

My aunties ain't grow
in no antebellum palace.
We come from those wood shacks
where Meshach's spirit still singing
in the wood stove.

We come from rust-coated
iron pots catching water
drops from tin roofs:
From tea cakes made from scratch,
and that ain't no jive.

Instead of going home from school,
I'd come see if you were sitting on the porch,
smoke curling like vines through the metal fence.
Before I could reach the gate,
you'd call it out—Hey Buckethead!
And I'd yell it right back.

I don't remember our last exchange,
but I know you said it.
I know I did too.
I know the smoke still lingers
when I walk past that house.
I wait, but there's no one left to say it back.

The box fan hums in the window,
its blades stirring thick summer heat,
not enough to cool the room,
but enough to try.

Life is in the things we forget to notice—
the whir of something working just enough,
it was never meant to be the breeze,
only the promise of it.

a cardinal sings
crimson against
an endless blue
song full of joy

Backwoods

I'm home behind loose wheels on backwood bends,
these mounds and curves won't take me out today.
Sunlight splits the tree line, slashing shadows,
cuts your white dress open at the seams.

Your fingers dig into my shoulder, firm,
your breath a tightrope waiting to give way.
The AC had a previous life and
refused resurrection, still, we chase heat.

No angels come looking this deep in the pines.
Eden ain't waiting where the road runs out—
just dust curling up behind us,
just your grip steadying my sins.
My little miss messiah wears waist beads:
Lays hands on me without a single prayer.

My drug of choice is isolation.

I forgot to call you back,
forgot we had a lunch date,
forgot to stop by the house—

but I never forgot your smile,
or your drive.

I only drank alone,
only reminisced in dark rooms.

I sat on a pew next to a man
I knew best when we were both boys.
I listened to your son deliver
words I could not form,
could not beat out of my knotted heart.

I was told strangers, to me, would carry you,
told where I wasn't needed,
told to stay strong.

I do not wish to be strong.

You told me, "It's not about what we want to do.
Sometimes it's about what we have to do."

You never told me
how to last longer than you.

Dear God,

Meet me out on Heaven's front porch
for a plate of souse 'n saltines.

I came to you young, Lord, 'bout ten
years old—Medea said that you spoke
during thunderstorms. She made us
take a nap but I stayed awake
just to hear your voice reign.

My tears might not crash on carpet the way
vibrations do in clouds—jukebox
worship, storm like music, my ear-
drums jubilant—but when I can
afford myself the time to cry,
I climb the stepladder.

Noise

I lost my cotton-picking mind,
or maybe I just set it down somewhere
between the pews and the porch light,
between the sermon and the Saturday night blues.

The pain was in the words,
but the vibrations just numb you to it.
Let the bassline hum, let the choir wail—
a sound so thick you can spread it on cornbread,
just let it sit heavy on your tongue.

My skin trembles when youth choirs moan,
songs pulled from the soul's innocent space
where the Lord lives, where He listens,
where He waits for us to stop singing
long enough to hear Him.

But I can't let it get that quiet yet.

And the Lord said,
Let there be laughter in the face of fear.
Let the congregation stand, unshaken.
Let a man sip from his cup and know
that the Spirit moves in more ways than one.

I don't read my Bible like I used to,
but I have studied His work—
just like my momma, and she pray with details.
Just like my uncle sip slow, he call it communion.
I know scripture:
I learned it best when the jukebox was preaching.

Some nights, I ask the Lord to let the locusts pass.
Other nights, I stand outside and wait for the swarm.
I ain't scared of you motherfuckers.
There ain't no promised land on this side of God,
but the liquor store stays open late.

October Nights

Tennessee Whiskey inhibits my ability
to feel the brisk air on October nights in Alabama.

I'm questioning my path again.
My momma sick,
but she'll stomach me.

Like a pathogen,
uncertainty spreads in our home.

Lines are blurred between lessons learned,
dreams deferred,
and spirits spilled to heal.

She's throwing stones but ain't killed me yet.
Jesus testing my patience.
Don't I pray?
Don't I isolate myself in the word
like a prisoner to faith?

A faith the devil wants me to cast away,
like a die against dim-lit corners,
end my life for the better—
as all the clutter between my shoulders divides me.

If my momma knew how wild I became,
would she still stomach me,
or am I abandoned to the moonlight
on October nights in Alabama?

A Silence We Both Kept

I wanted to pray to God—
ask Him to take away your pain—
then bit my tongue,
realizing your mission was the same.
Your death would haunt my days
And settle in my bones at night.
We work this field in silence.
Something heavy lingers in the air,
Like rain that never comes.
I watch you take breaths.

An angel arrived—
told me to be still.
To let go.
And when I did,
roots curled into my veins,
and the wind tucked itself
beneath my ribs.
I was no longer alone.
I was the earth.

the doctor says my eyes might die.
that they forget how to hold each other.
that the words might double.
that I will have to pull them together
and live through the blur.

he says it so lightly—
as if it's nothing. as if I wont
pluck them
from my skull myself,
if the decay attempts to spread.

Warmth

Tears fall,
but there is no audience here—
only darkness
to cradle them,
only quiet.

And somewhere in it,
between breath and ache,
the world still holds warmth
just for you.

Island

I didn't know I was on an island
until my soul peeked
out its window to spy on all the
truth the world knew.

I could see the shades of
lament that shackled me,
painted with weight around
my neck and wrist.

Never found any kegs to
free myself—only a box with
a sailor's jacket that had
"Adventure" stitched on its lapel,
still waiting to be worn.

Splash. Splash. Splash.

The boy flailed in the lake,
water clawing at his skin.
Fish fled to the shadows.
The man on the shore
watched—
unmoved.

Each time the boy surfaced,
gasping, he caught glimpses
of the world beyond the water—
autumn leaves drifting lazily downward,
crickets shifting in the brush,
the sky stretching vast and indifferent.

Splash. Splash. Splash.

His arms burned,
his chest tightened.
The shore seemed so far away.
The body tires before the will does.
He sank.

Cold wrapped around him,
pulled him deeper,
silenced the world above.
For a moment, he felt peace—
the quiet hum of surrender.

Then—hands.

He was lifted, dragged to the shore,
the ground rough beneath his back.
Air filled his lungs,
but his body no longer belonged to him.
He did not shiver.
He did not fight.

The man knelt beside him,
His expression did not change.
The boy stared at him,
then at the lake,
then at the sky.

He knew what came next.
He stood,
walked back to the edge,
stepped forward.

The water opened for him.
Splash. Splash. Splash.

Lies—

they sprout from black-hearted roots,
a rose growing wild in the wrong garden.
Even when the truth comes,
you hold onto the lies that gave you peace,
but they only give you pain.

Lies bring

pain.
You try to hold them in your mouth,
but they spill, thick as blood,
pooling in the cracks between your teeth.
You tell the mirror, but mirrors can't be trusted.
They only throw your reflection back at you.

Lies bring

tears.
Even the strongest man flinches at truths he hides.
I visit the headstones of my best memories,
before lies showed they weren't my friends.
I sit with what's left of yesterday.

Cacoethes

I must live the life I was given,
even if it unravels me.
What else is living for,
if not to burn through one life
so I might live again?
To breathe existence instead of air,
to touch love, to taste death—
to see the future rush toward me
without knowing where my heart belongs.

Path

Hands on the wheel's rim—
the unyielding road ahead
steers itself alone.

Flash

the siren woke me

racing to bodies near bloodstained
white walls in a house on 53rd,
a seven-car pileup on Highland,
two homicides, opposite ends of town—

the siren woke me.

even though those lights encourage drifting
away, momentary flashes cut through silence,
distracting us from the fact that the sick and dying
never wait in traffic.

Storm

Storms are not humane.
They will toss you, leave you wrecked—
break, then break again.

One Pull

I have rested on the wall,
but I was never meant for display.
His hands find me like habit,
like a wave to a neighbor
crossing his path.

I am not cold in his grasp.
I am waiting.
His movements are careful,
but I have never known hesitation.
One held breath, one pull,
and I am singing again—
take space like a cicada's call.

Then I sleep again,
back on the wall,
listening for the next fool
who don't know what waits in the dark.

The moon watches me.
I watch it back.
The branches try
to break the stare,
but they fail.
I breathe in the night,
let it settle in my bones.
I could do this forever.
But morning comes,
stealing the night
before I'm ready
to let it go.

Track Junkie

I
stand in
a quiet place surrounded
by fading echoes
of men encased with wax.
See eyes following me, heads tilted,
the hairs on my arms
fall back into place—
they are the messengers of my addiction,
tell me the silence is
overrated,
each measure to incite
snaps and crackles,
appeal only to heartstrings.
I draw the needle
with my fingertips,
it scratches the surface,
and the quiet place becomes noise.
My arm hairs give ovation,
and this new track
makes me feel
alive.

I'm only alive when I'm moving.
The money chase pulls me, has
wrapped up my dreams in altitude—
bound them to the climb.
And now the fall feels inevitable.

I crash hard.
Still, there is something in me
that is reaching, that refuses
to sink. I will ascend again.

Blank

Sitting
at my desk,
I contemplated
writing that sad poem
just because I was shedding
a few tears, but what's the use
drenching this paper with pain
that will soon dry and leave
the page just as blank
as it was before?

In or Out

The rules here are the same as yo' momma's house—
you gotta stay in or stay out of my heart.

See, my heart swings like a southern screen door,
opens slow, closes heavy.
The hinges might creak, might resist,
but it don't stay open long.

You will not track dirt in here, ma'am.
I ain't got space for footprints I didn't invite.
Ain't no rug, ain't no towel by the door,
just bare floor—hardwood before you reach carpet.

When the streetlights hum and the night calls you back,
I won't be standing on the porch calling your name.
The lock turns easy at ten o'clock sharp.

Just like at yo' momma's house,
my heart got rules.
And I ain't one for second chances.

The love was warm...

and even though it ended,
even though we unraveled,
I still carry the threads.

No Soft Landings

Your touch got weight—
you trace your fingers down my spine,
but you ain't looking at me.
Not really.
Your hands know a body, not a man.

I move careful these days,
started looking both ways crossing one-way streets,
started walking backwards,
like maybe I could unmake the moments
where love was just something
that happened to me,
not something I held in my own hands.

You don't see me.
Not really.
But you still pull me closer,
and I let you,
because some nights, there ain't no soft landings.
No open arms, no gentle undoing.
Just bodies tangled in the weight of their wanting,
just hands gripping for something steady,
just the slow collapse of two people
who never learned how to fall softly.

I Know What I Am

Fuck my intentions—
I'm selfish.

I come on strong,
but I can tell
you're trying to rekindle innocence.

Your flame fights for oxygen
I planned on stealing
from your lips
until I felt its warmth.

Now I wonder—
was I ever drawn to you,
or just to the light?

Lust Deferred

What happens to a lust deferred?
Does it dry up, crack open,
spill itself back into the earth?

You make me want to sow my seeds
in your fertile soil,
but I know better.
Ain't nothing here that's meant to bloom.

Baton Rouge

A taste of her makes the blood rush,
a slow burn, a red pepper heat,
undertones of Tony's lingers
on my tongue, wild and unshaken.

Southern eyes,
a mouth that don't know how to be mild.
I chase fire now, and there ain't no point
pretending I could ever go back
to a bland loving.

Who said hunger ain't reason enough?
Who said craving is a crime?
My heart remember the heat—
a fire that don't ask permission to burn.

Distance

I count the seconds, the miles, the space
between your breath and mine.

Lie in my arms again.
Whisper the ways you want to be touched
until your sighs betray your judgment.

I curse the pavement, the empty road,
every stretch of highway that separates us.
I'd wear out my soles just to see you smile.

Under a glassy, starlit sky,
we drift further but somehow closer—
counting laughs, heartbreaks, the weight of waiting
until yesterday fades into today.

Woman, I don't care how far you are.
I'm coming.

Would you climb this peak
just to see my hidden face?
Or leave me waiting?

When the reaper came,
I never heard your last breath.
Friendship died silent.

You think you know me
but your own reflection lies—
we changed long ago.

speak loud
when you speak
love to me

My culture lives in barbershops,
where old heads congregate
from sun-up till sun-down,
till "Son, listen here."

Where word is born,
and the length of the shop is a stage
for the layman's cause.

Where script is scripture,
and front stage ain't gospel
unless there's good news from the back.

The Weight of You

They don't celebrate much round here, unc,
But life.
Keep funeral devices packed like nightclubs,
Dressed to the nines,
This the ninth one this month.
Tried to drink myself numb,
Yet I still feel the open air you stood in.
Now you lie there.
You don't look like Busta—
Too shiny,
Not like you could teach a boy to shake hands,
Grip tight and stiff,
Like the weight of you in this damn box.
Too shiny.
You been processed,
Refurbished,
And offered to us.
My suit is too tight.
The air too thick.
Your name is heavy in the preacher's mouth.
I'm still searching for myself
In the loudness of your memory

Letters from a Witness

Dear God,

It's hot outside.

It's hot and heaven ain't shedin' tears like it used to,
and I think it's because the King of Love is dead.
He died when the ground was damp—
they killed him because he believed in that shit,
and we believed him when he said,

"Hate cannot drive out hate,
only love can do that."

Goddamn, everyone knows about Memphis.

Dear God,

It's hot outside.

It's hot because the Sun ain't nonviolent.
I keep trying to rally prayers for rain,
but it don't work. So instead, I'm beggin' you—
beggin' you to reign the Sun in,
or let 'em step up off heaven's stoop to fight me.
I got Detroit Red in my ear, yelling,

"We are only nonviolent
with people who are nonviolent with us."

Goddamn, everyone knows about Manhattan,
and Goddammit, they know about Chicago too.

What about next time?

Dear God,

It's still hot outside.

It's hot and there's no more water—
like my Medea used to sing—
no more water,
and these times got me so upset
with this janky concept of freedom.

Right and wrong seem so black and white,
yet so white and black in practice.

They abandoned you.

I knew they abandoned you when I read
that they were burning crosses to make statements.
Well, what will they burn next time?

Dear God,

We started burning courts and police buildings.
To make statements:

Because everyone knows about Minneapolis.

It's hotter outside, and now the earth is parched—
no more water.
I'll die here next time
before all they get is a witness.

The Ash

It came on trains from Tennessee,
extracted from the Emory River,
express to Perry County—
dumped and forgotten in the dirt that raised me.

I grew tired of hearing rails rumble,
watching elders sip Jack Daniel's,
as if whiskey would deafen the whistle
that signaled the sickness arriving
again, and again.

The ash flakes taint my memories—
picking jujubees from vines
that echo stories of the town.

But that black soil ain't yield a weak people.
A people rediscovered their purple claws
and golden strength.

A people won't be pelted by arrowheads
uncontested. A people breathe despite.
A people exhale.

Rebellion

My country is a roaring ocean,
a crowd longing to see me broken,
to see me rise in the tide,
to see my fall.

I am American,
by way of auction blocks,
by way of the world's stage,
questioning my entrance
on such stony waters.

Yet you think the greatest pain
is to die.

In the old age,
Black was not counted fair.
Black forgot its passions in the dread,
unable to fight,
or else be beaten.

Be broken men with no spirit to live,
broken women with no soul to pass down.

Curtains close before the fourth act sounds,
at the signal of white-back vultures
who pick at the bones of the old age.

Yet you think the greatest pain
is to die.

speak,
but only in whispers—
to make them lean in,
to make them listen.

then yell.

They tell us
to trust our leaders.
War tells us
what their words won't.
March on.
Follow the flag.
Keep your head low.
Kill where they tell you.
Swallow your soul
before it swallows you.
March on.
March on.
And let the past
be forgotten.

We were taught
to believe in the dream—
American Dream.
It was a fiction
written in blood.
I know it was the blood.
I know it was the blood.
I know it was the blood
of the dreamers.

Dear Black man,

I see your will
fluctuate while
you fight the world—
a world that attached the sin
to your melanin.

Ain't never treated
you like a child
of any man's god.

I am not a name

I am not a name,
nor a color, nor a box.
I am something more.

switch hats
to match the crowd,
hoping they won't see
the weight you
carry underneath?
Do you think
a brim low enough
can hide the parts
of yourself
you don't want them to see?

Black is not…

Black is not my end.
Black is the ground where I stand,
the roots and the sky.

Son of the Right Hand

I was meant to kneel,
meant to shield,
meant to whisper wisdom
to the one who held the throne.
But shadows stretch at dusk,
and I have waited for the light to shift.
Tonight, I do not kneel.
Tonight, I do not wait for a pardon.
The crown will not be given;
it will be eaten by wolves.

They called it revolution
but sold it in ticket stubs.

A body framed in gold chains,
a soundtrack of funk and gunfire.
Black skin lit like a neon ad—
cool, dangerous,
profitable.

They never asked if we wanted to be heroes.
They just gave us scripts
and a quota.

So, we played the role.
Spoke through gritted teeth,
walked like vengeance wrapped in leather.
Made them love the menace
they swore they feared.

They handed us guns,
and we turned them on the screen.
Allowed our rage:
let the world think we had none left for them.

They never asked if we wanted to be heroes.
So, we became something else.

Label a child bad and put them in a corner.

Quiet corners began to take hold of them.
They trade tethers to quiet corners
for tethers to street corners,
screaming "fuck twelve" since twelve.
Street corners become cells inside state-funded
buildings.

If the only light comes from ceilings they can't reach,
they pray for coroners
to replace their label with a toe tag.

Freedom

So far from me,
shackled in my own heart.
Emotions locked away,
common sense reigning like a warden.

Yet I wish for—
freedom.

Freedom
to speak real,
to let the heart say
what the mouth always swallows.

To breathe without permission.
To exist without apology.

Freedom.

About the Author

Benjamin Jackson (Ben) is a writer from Uniontown, Alabama, whose love for words started in church. At St. Peter Primitive Baptist, instead of reading the pre-made speeches for youth programs, he was encouraged by his mother, Rosetta King, to write his own—his first taste of shaping language to fit his voice.

Ben is an alumnus of R.C. Hatch High School but spent a year at the Alabama School of Math & Science, where he turned to poetry as a way to cope with the pressures of a more demanding academic environment.

He grew up in a culture shaped by the Civil Rights Movement, but in high school, that history became more than just stories from the past. While his father, Rev. James E. Jackson Sr., pastored Brown Chapel A.M.E. in Selma—a church deeply woven into the movement's legacy—Ben began to understand its impact in a more personal way. That influence only deepened when he moved to Selma for college, where he was surrounded by the city's history and the people who had lived it.

While in Selma, he earned his associate's degree and later transferred to the University of Montevallo. Initially an English major, he stepped away from school for three years before returning, drawn to Sociology instead. With the guidance of trusted professors, he found a new way to connect his love of storytelling with understanding people, earning a Bachelor of Science with a minor in writing.

Since then, Ben has worked with nonprofits focused on improving the lives of people in Alabama's Black Belt and supporting Black entrepreneurs in the Birmingham metro area. His work is rooted in the South, shaped by history, memory, and the everyday lives of the people and places that raised him.